ANO PLAY-ALONG

FRANK SINATRA
POPULAR HITS

CONTENTS

PAGE	TITLE	DEMO TRACK	PLAY-ALONG TRACK
2	Come Fly with Me	1	9
8	Cycles	2	10
12	High Hopes	3	11
15	Love and Marriage	4	12
18	My Way	5	13
23	Strangers in the Night	6	14
26	(Love Is) The Tender Trap	7	15
30	Young at Heart	8	16

Cover photo courtesy of Photofest

ISBN-13: 978-1-4234-0497-2
ISBN-10: 1-4234-0497-1

HAL•LEONARD®
CORPORATION
7777 W. BLUEMOUND RD. P.O. BOX 13819 MILWAUKEE, WI 53213

Visit Hal Leonard Online at
www.halleonard.com

COME FLY WITH ME

Words by SAMMY CAHN
Music by JAMES VAN HEUSEN

Moderately slow

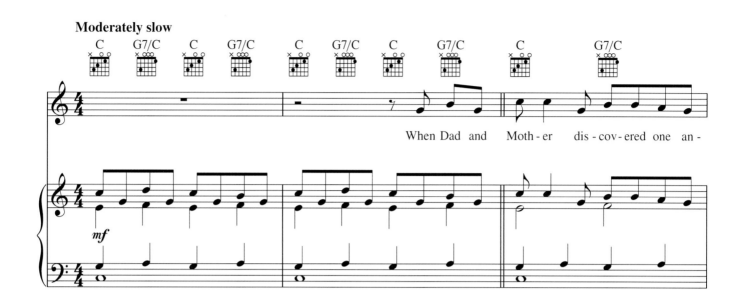

When Dad and Moth-er dis-cov-ered one an-

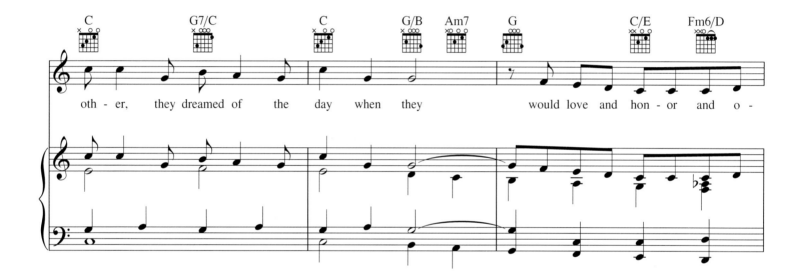

oth-er, they dreamed of the day when they would love and hon-or and o-

bey, and dur-ing all their mod-est spoon-ing,

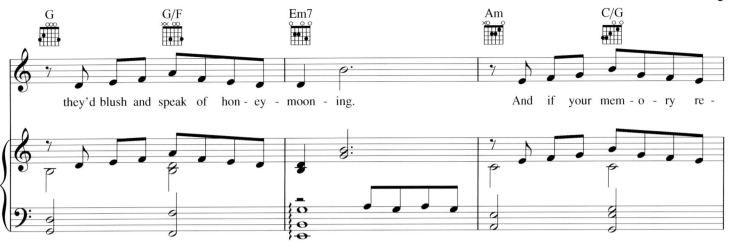

they'd blush and speak of hon-ey-moon-ing. And if your mem-o-ry re-

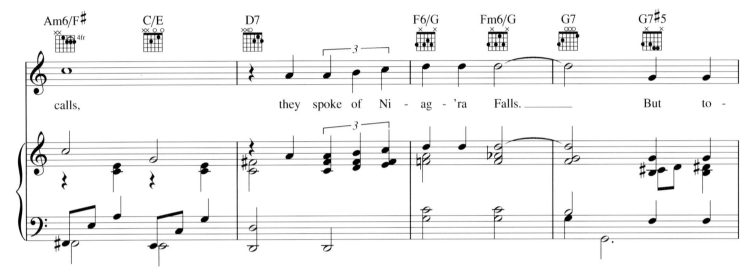

calls, they spoke of Ni-ag-'ra Falls. _____ But to-

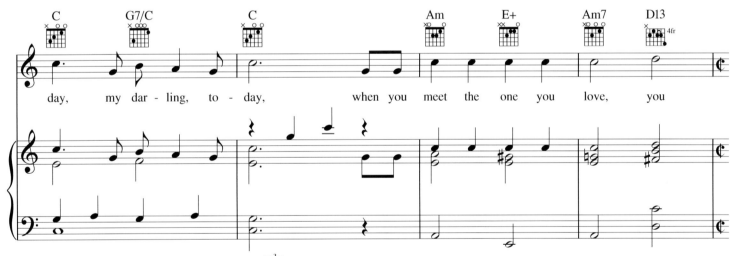

day, my dar-ling, to-day, when you meet the one you love, you

Moderately, with a strong beat

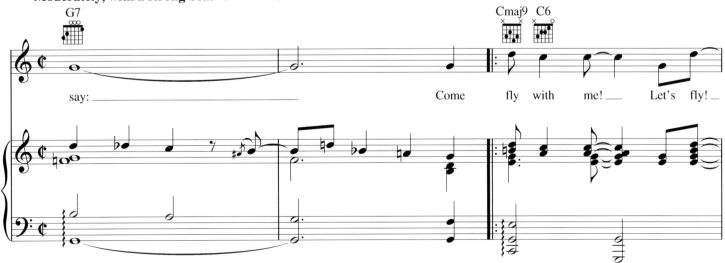

say: _____ Come fly with me! __ Let's fly! __

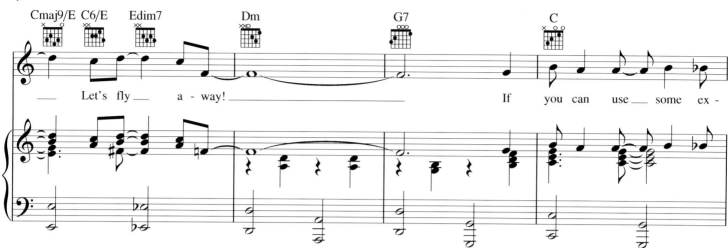

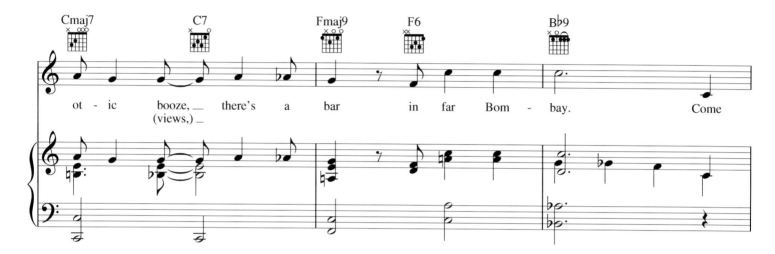

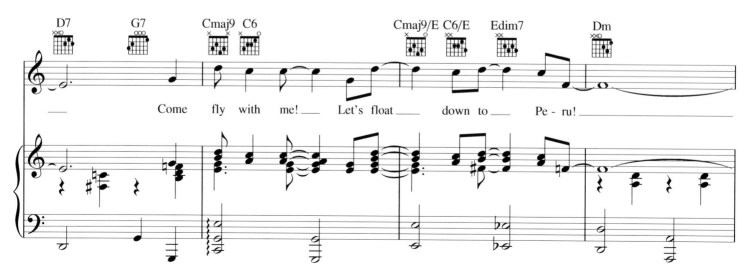

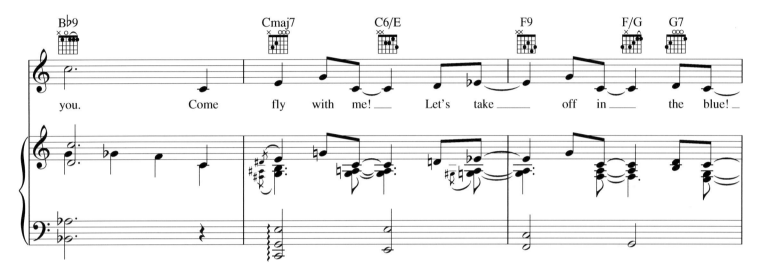

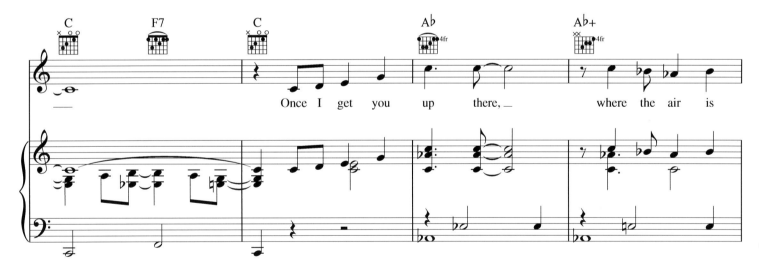

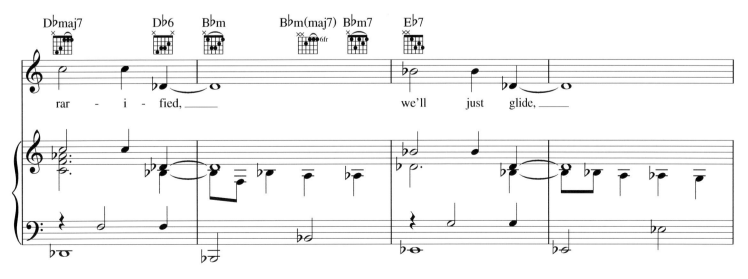

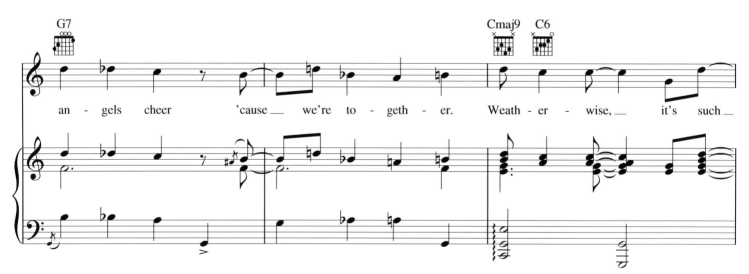

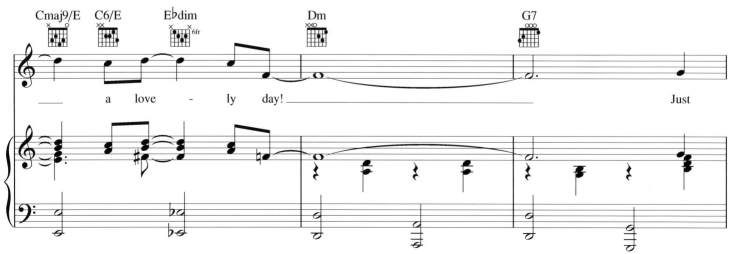

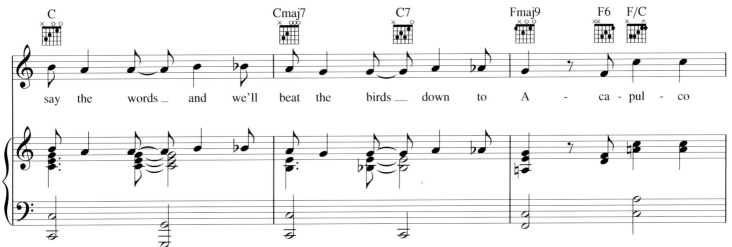

say the words___ and we'll beat the birds___ down to A - ca - pul - co

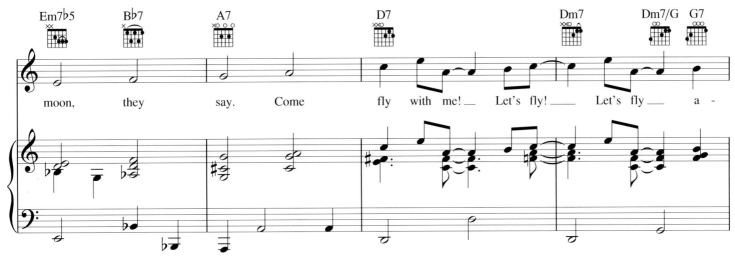

Bay. It's per - fect for___ a fly - ing hon - ey -

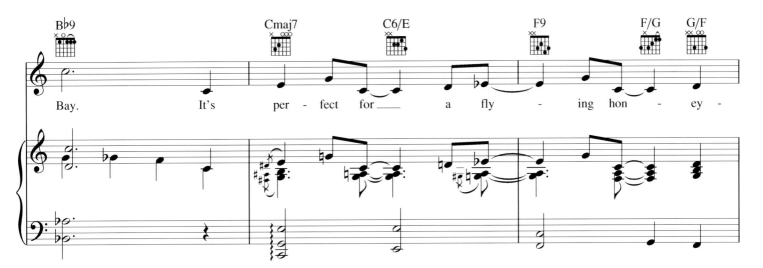

moon, they say. Come fly with me!___ Let's fly!___ Let's fly___ a -

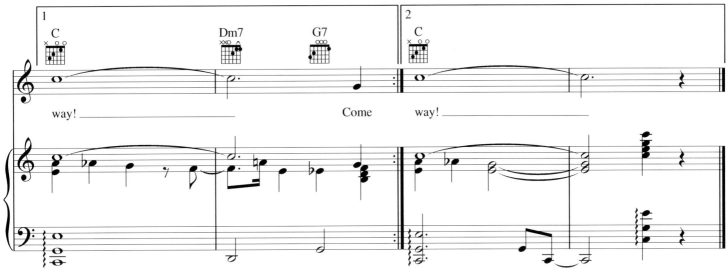

way!_____ Come way!_____

CYCLES

Words and Music by
GAYLE CALDWELL

brings. _____

true. _____

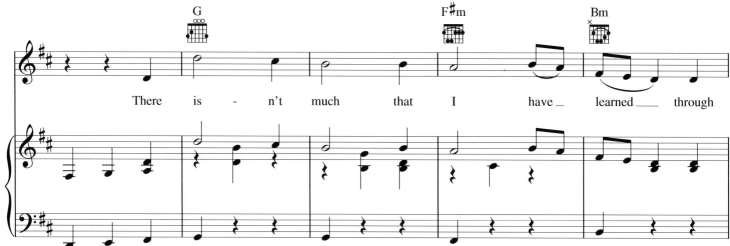

There is - n't much that I have __ learned ___ through

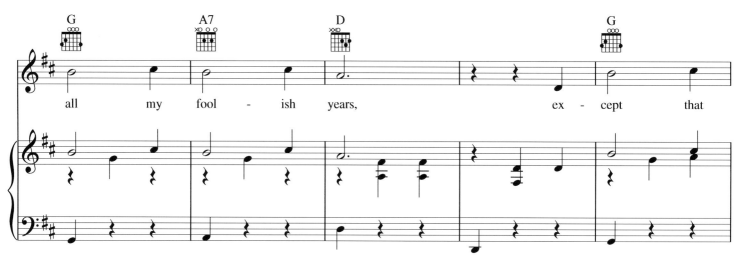

all my fool - ish years, ex - cept that

life keeps run - nin' ___ in ___ cy - cles.

First, there's laugh-ter, then there's tears. _____

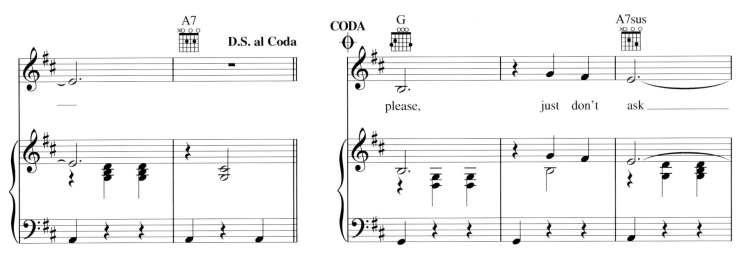

D.S. al Coda

CODA

please, just don't ask _____

me now. _____

Optional Ending

Repeat and Fade

HIGH HOPES

Words by SAMMY CAHN
Music by JAMES VAN HEUSEN

Moderately, with a beat

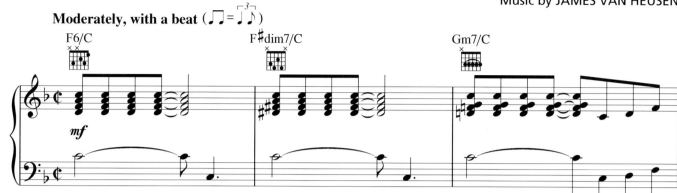

Next time you're found _ with your chin on the ground, _ there's a
When trou-bles call _ and your back's to the wall, _ there's a
Instrumental

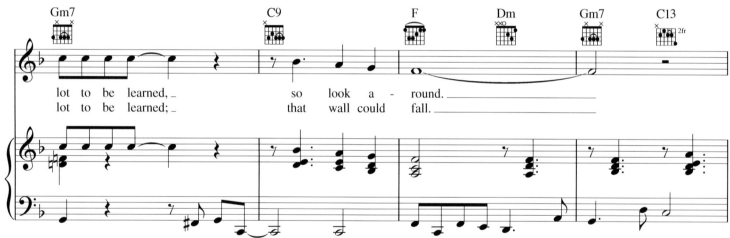

lot to be learned, _ so look a - round.
lot to be learned; _ that wall could fall. _____

Just what makes that lit-tle ol' ant _ think he'll move that rub-ber tree plant.
Once there was a sil-ly ol' ram, _ thought he'd punch a hole in a dam.

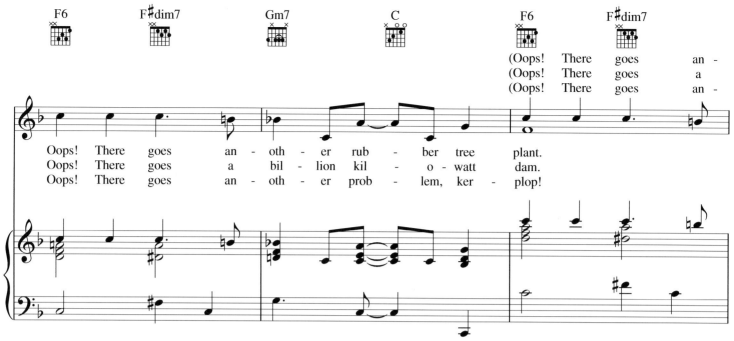

(Oops! There goes an a-
(Oops! There goes a
(Oops! There goes an-

Oops! There goes an - oth - er rub - ber tree plant.
Oops! There goes a bil - lion kil - o - watt dam.
Oops! There goes an - oth - er prob - lem, ker - plop!

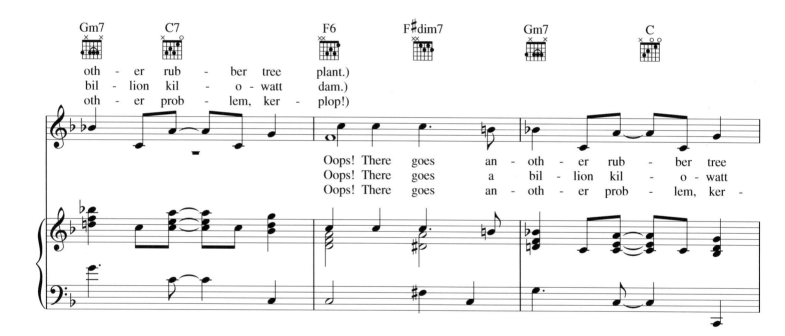

oth - er rub - ber tree plant.)
bil - lion kil - o - watt dam.)
oth - er prob - lem, ker - plop!)

Oops! There goes an - oth - er rub - ber tree
Oops! There goes a bil - lion kil - o - watt
Oops! There goes an - oth - er prob - lem, ker -

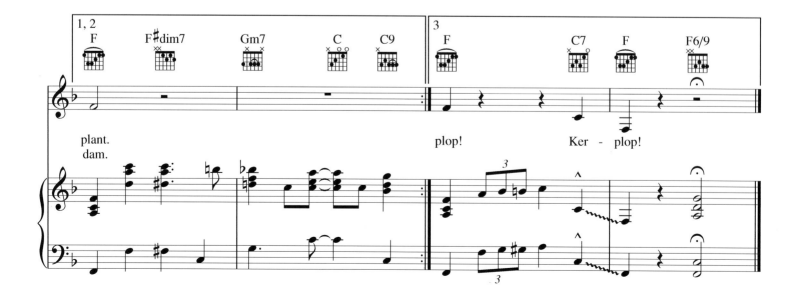

plant.
dam.

plop! Ker - plop!

LOVE AND MARRIAGE

Words by SAMMY CAHN
Music by JAMES VAN HEUSEN

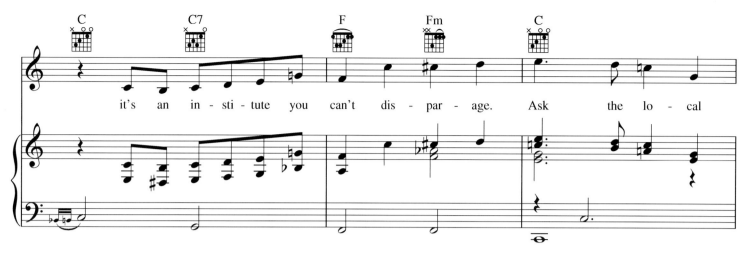

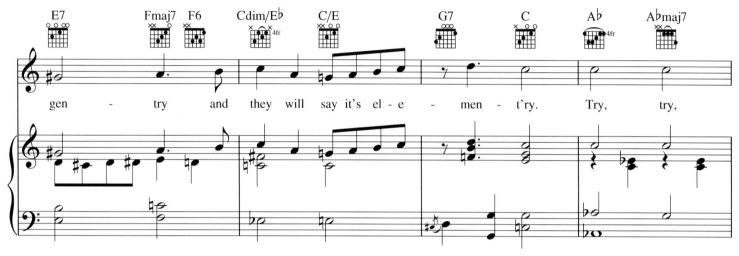

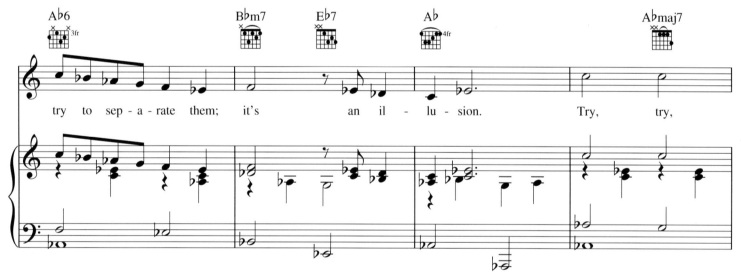

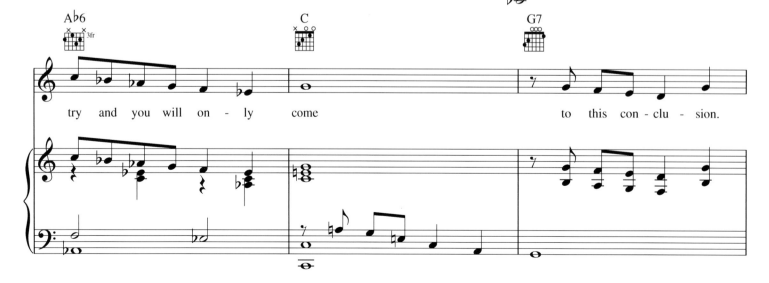

MY WAY

English Words by PAUL ANKA
Original French Words by GILLES THIBAULT
Music by JACQUES REVAUX
and CLAUDE FRANCOIS

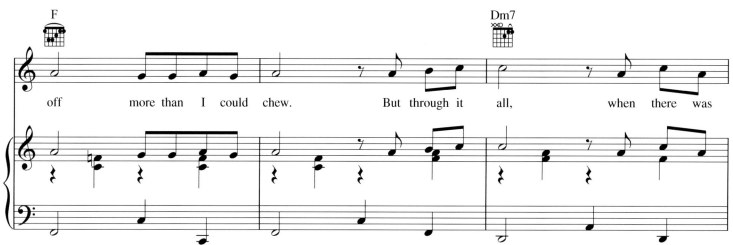

off   more than I could chew.   But through it all,   when there was

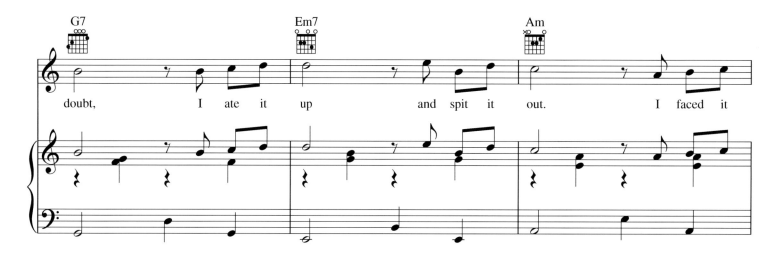

doubt,   I ate it up   and spit it out.   I faced it

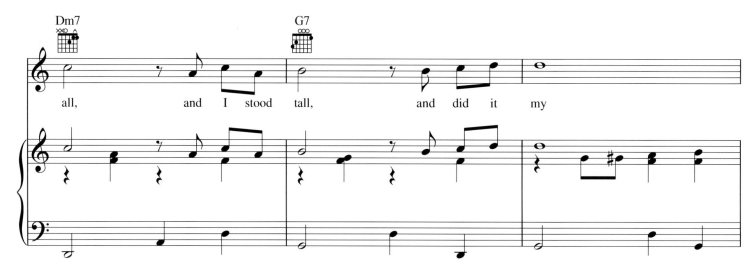

all,   and I stood tall,   and did it my

way.   I've loved,   I've laughed and cried,   I've had my

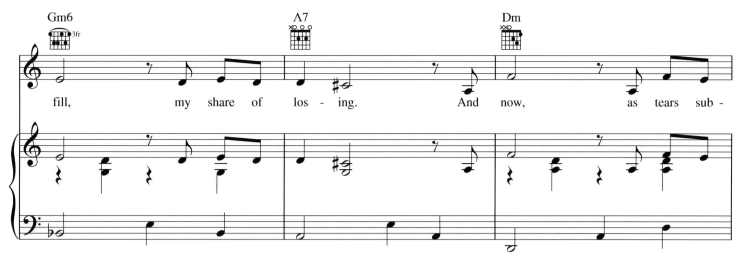

fill, my share of los - ing. And now, as tears sub -

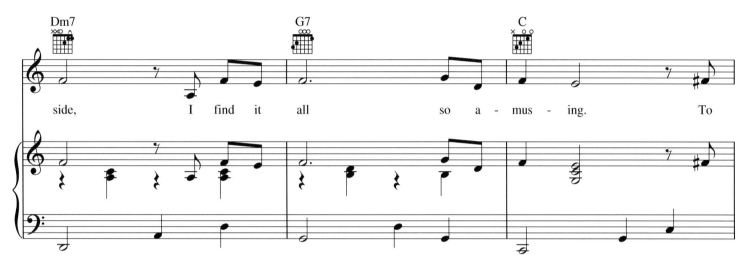

side, I find it all so a - mus - ing. To

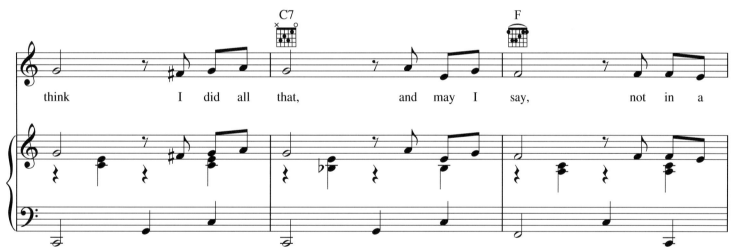

think I did all that, and may I say, not in a

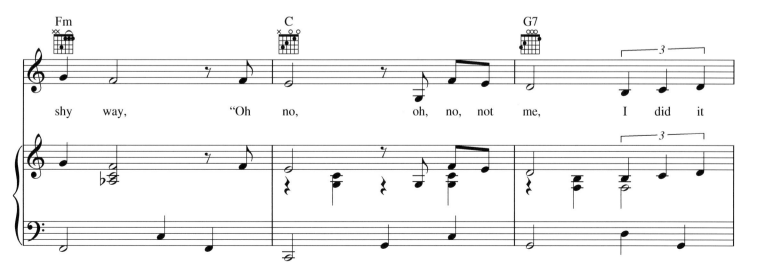

shy way, "Oh no, oh, no, not me, I did it

my way." For what is a man, what has he got? If not him-

self, then he has naught. To say the things he tru-ly

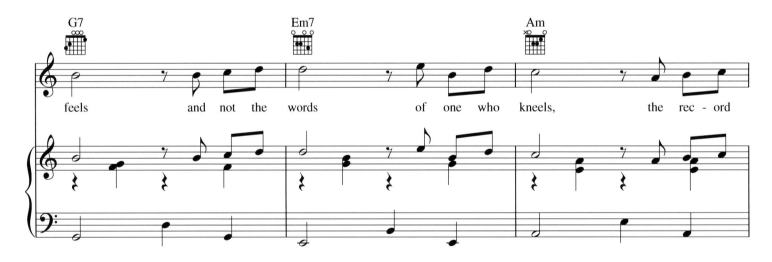

feels and not the words of one who kneels, the rec-ord

shows I took the blows, and did it my way.

STRANGERS IN THE NIGHT
adapted from A MAN COULD GET KILLED

Words by CHARLES SINGLETON
and EDDIE SNYDER
Music by BERT KAEMPFERT

(Love Is)
THE TENDER TRAP

Words by SAMMY CAHN
Music by JAMES VAN HEUSEN

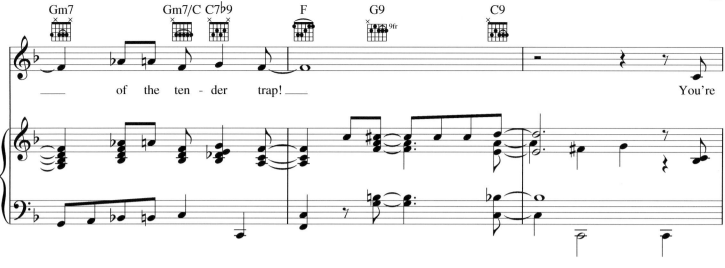

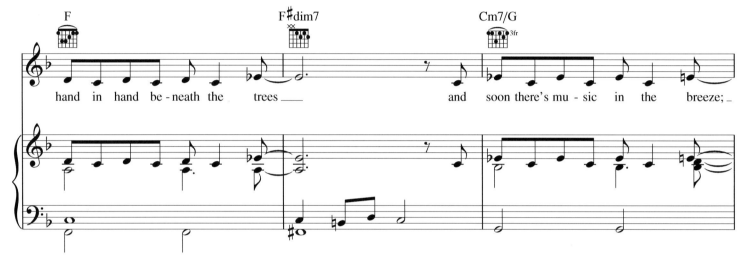

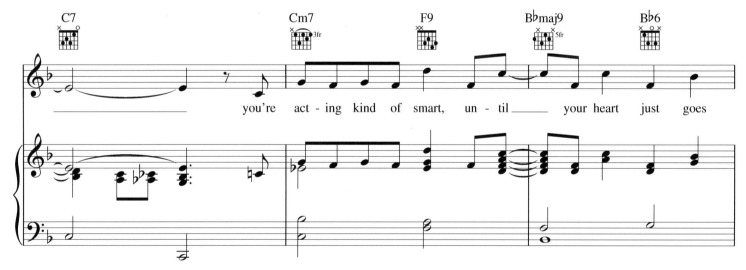

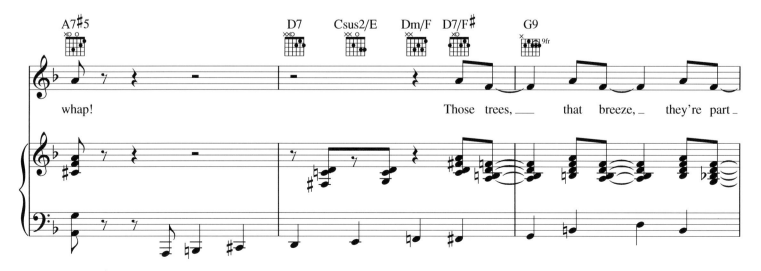

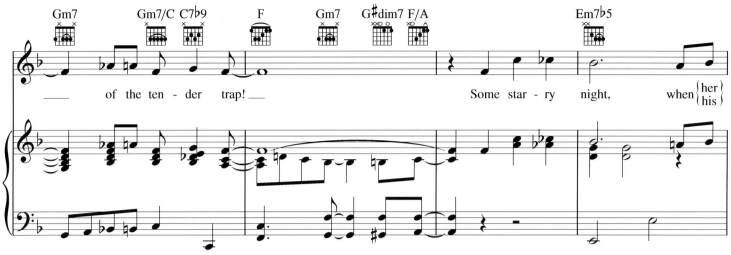

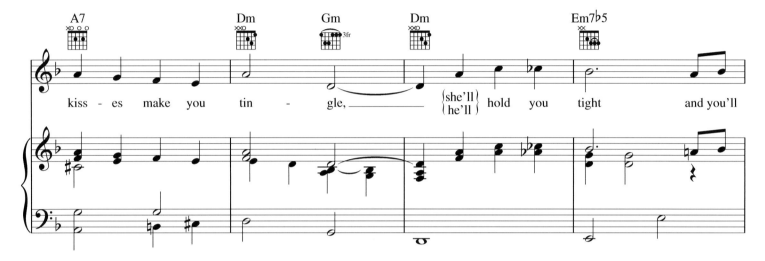

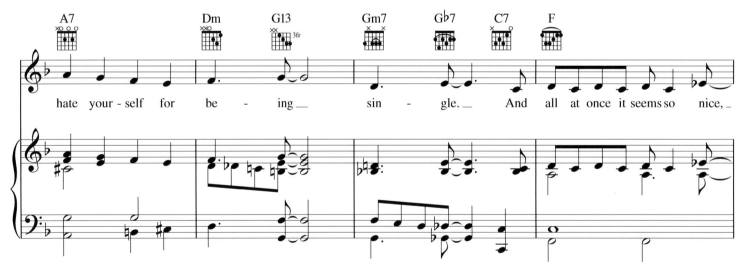

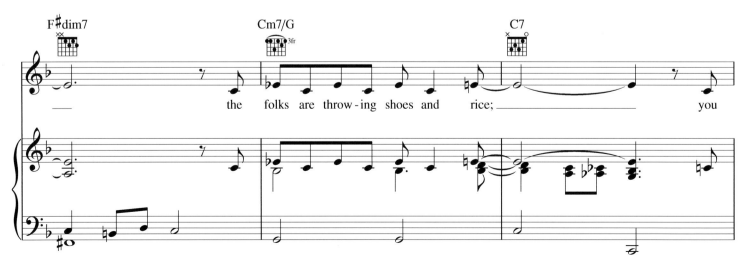

YOUNG AT HEART

from YOUNG AT HEART

Words by CAROLYN LEIGH
Music by JOHNNY RICHARDS

Fair-y tales can come true, it can hap-pen to you if you're

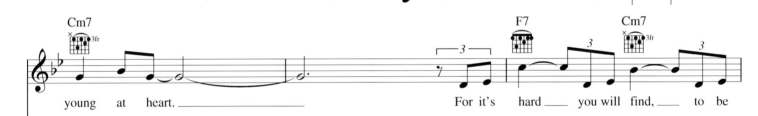

young at heart. For it's hard you will find, to be

nar-row of mind if you're young at heart. You can